Table of Contents

Introduction

Gastric bypass is surgery that helps you lose weight by changing how your stomach and small intestine handle the food you eat.

After the surgery, your stomach will be smaller. You will feel full with less food. The food you eat will no longer go into some parts of your stomach and small intestine that absorb food. Because of this, your body will not get all of the calories from the food you eat.

Therefore, your new diet helps you progress with weight loss in a nutritionally sound manner to reach your health goals. Eating a variety of foods will help you obtain adequate protein, vitamins and minerals.

In view of this, this book contains 25 healthy bariatric recipes with an easy guide on a how to prepare them for your weight loss surgery diet.

Here Are the List of Bariatric Recipes

Garlic Lemon Shrimp Kabobs

Kabobs are the ultimate single-serving food. It doesn't get much simpler than that. Using lean shrimp makes this recipe standout because it's basically pure protein and calculable. Add these to a salad or eat them on their own, either way, these will keep you on track with your bariatric diet.

Ingredients

- 1.33 lbs shrimp, peeled and deveined

- Salt and pepper

- 2 tbsp butter, melted

- 1/4 cup freshly squeezed lemon juice

- 4 cloves garlic, minced

- 1 tsp Italian seasoning

- 2 tbsp parsley, chopped

Instructions

1. Preheat the oven to 450 degrees or preheat the grill.

2. Add the butter to a small saucepan. Once it melts, add the garlic, lemon juice, and Italian seasoning.

3. Cook for 2-3 minutes on low until garlic is fragrant.

4. Thread the shrimp on skewers. Season with salt and pepper. To cook in the oven, place on a baking sheet and cook for 5-6 minutes until pink and cooked through.

5. To cook on the grill, place directly on the grill and cook for 2-3 minutes per side until opaque and cooked through.

6. When the shrimp are cooked, brush with the garlic butter mixture and serve.

Ancho Chile Ground Beef Tacos

Street tacos are normally fried in oil and contain fatty versions of meat with vegetables fried in oils. This makes for some seriously high-fat (small) tacos that leave you hungry and needing more food. This version make use of lean ground beef and seasonings for flavor to keep the calorie count low and the flavor high.

Ingredients

- 1 tbsp. ancho chile powder
- 1/2 tbsp. cumin
- 1/2 tsp. smoked paprika
- 1/2 tbsp. oregano

- 1/2 tbsp. garlic powder

- 1/2 tbsp. onion powder

- 1/2 tsp. coriander

- 1/2 tsp. salt

- 1/2 tsp. pepper

- 1 lb. 95% lean ground beef

- 1/3 cup water

- 1/2 tbsp. cornstarch

Instructions

1. Mix together ancho chili powder, cumin, paprika, oregano, garlic powder, onion powder, coriander, salt, and pepper. This

makes a delicious homemade taco seasoning.

2. Brown the beef (or turkey) in a skillet until cooked through. Drain any excess fat. If you like you could add vegetables during this step you could – diced onions, red and yellow peppers, canned and drained diced tomatoes, or diced zucchini would be delicious. Beans are also a delicious addition.

3. Whisk together the water and cornstarch.

4. Add to the pan along with the taco seasoning and bring to a simmer. Let simmer for 3-4 minutes until sauce thickens.

Boom Bang-a-Bang Chicken Cups

This healthy supper is super speedy - top lettuce leaves with cooked chicken, colourful vegetables and a peanut and sweet chilli sauce.

Ingredients

- 100g smooth peanut butter
- 140g full-fat coconut yogurt or natural yogurt mixed with 2 tbsp desiccated coconut
- 2 tsp sweet chilli sauce
- 2 tsp soy sauce
- 2-3 spring onions finely shredded
- 3 cooked skinless chicken breasts, shredded
- 2 Baby Gem lettuces, big leaves separated

- ½ cucumber, halved lengthways, seeds scraped out with a teaspoon, cut into matchsticks
- toasted sesame seeds, for sprinkling

Instructions

1. In your smallest pan, gently warm peanut butter, yogurt, 3 tbsp water, sweet chili and soy sauce until melted together into a smooth sauce. Set aside and allow to cool.

2. Mix the spring onions and chicken into the sauce and season. Chill until the party. Keep the lettuce leaves and cucumber under damp kitchen paper.

3. To assemble, add a bundle of cucumber to each lettuce leaf cup, plus a spoonful of the chicken mixture.

4. Sprinkle with sesame seeds and sit on a big platter for everyone to dig in. Or simply serve a pile of lettuce leaves alongside bowls of chicken and cucumber.

Buffalo Chicken Cups

Can we enjoy the taste of buffalo wings and still lose weight? Of course we can. This recipe takes lean chicken and delicious buffalo sauce to create a myriad of sinfully delicious flavors. These will be your new favorite over even the traditional hot wings!

Ingredients

- 2-3 boneless, skinless chicken breasts

- 2 Tbsp. olive oil

- 1/2 tsp. smoked paprika

- 1/2 tsp. chili powder

- 24 wonton wrappers

- 1 Tbsp. butter, melted

- 1/2 cup cayenne hot sauce

- 1/2 cup blue cheese crumbles

- 3 scallions, sliced thinly

Instructions

1. Preheat oven to 350F degrees.

2. Brush chicken breasts with olive oil, and then sprinkle evenly with smoked paprika and chili powder.

3. Place in a baking dish and cook for 20-30 minutes, or until the center is no longer pink and the juices run clear.

4. Remove chicken and let cool, then shred.

5. Meanwhile, fit a wonton wrapper into each of 24 mini baking cups, pressing the wrappers carefully but firmly into sides of cups.

Note: Be careful to keep the corners of each wonton wrapper open; otherwise you will not be able to fill them.

6. Bake for 5 minutes or until very lightly browned. Keep wontons in baking cups.

7. In a medium-sized bowl, stir together the melted butter and hot sauce.

8. Add the chicken and stir until well coated. Then fill each wonton cup with a tablespoon or two of chicken, and then top with a pinch of blue cheese.

9. Return wonton cups to oven and cook for another 5-10 minutes, or until cheese is soft and melty.

10. Remove and top with sliced scallions, and
serve warm. These are best served
immediately.

Thai Chicken Salad Wonton Cups

Chicken can be so versatile and that is apparent in
this delicious chicken salad cup. The wonton cup
gives the necessary crunch to the salad. The lime
and sesame seeds really give this the distinct Thai
flavor you are sure to love.

Ingredients

- 12 wonton wrappers

Dressing:

- 1 garlic, smashed

- 1½ tbsp lime juice

- 2 tsp rice vinegar

- 2½ tsp fish sauce

- 1 tsp soy sauce

- 1½ tbsp canola oil (or grape seed, vegetable or other neutral flavoured oil)

- 1 tsp sugar (or honey)

- 1 – 2 birds eye chilli, deseeded and finely chopped (or 1 – 2 tsp of chili paste or hot sauce)

Chicken Salad:

- 1½ cups shredded cooked chicken

- 1½ cups finely shredded cabbage

- ¾ cup carrot, finely julienned

- ⅓ cup finely chopped shallots/scallions

Garnish:

- Sesame seeds

- Fresh coriander/cilantro leaves

Instructions

1. Preheat oven to 160C/320F.

2. Place wonton wrappers into a regular muffin

   tin, moulding it into the cups.

3. Bake for 12 to 15 minutes, until crisp and light golden brown.

4. Remove from the oven and let the cups cool in the muffin tin.

5. Store in an airtight container until required (stays crisp for up to 3 days).

6. Combine Dressing ingredients in a jar and shake to combine.

7. Set aside for at least 10 minutes to allow the flavours to infuse.

8. Combine Chicken Salad ingredients in a bowl and toss to combine.

9. **To serve:** Discard the garlic clove from the Dressing, then toss it through the Chicken Salad.

10. Divide the Chicken Salad between the cups. Garnish with sesame seeds and cilantro/coriander, if using.

11. Serve immediately.

Crab Salad in Crisp Wonton Cup

We need variety in our diets, otherwise we get burnt out on foods we may even love and have loved for years. Chicken and beef are great, but we need an offering from the sea to round out our diet. These crab salad cups are just what you need if you're missing that taste of the ocean.

Ingredients

For the Wonton Cups:

- Cooking spray

- 18 wonton wrappers

- 2 teaspoons canola oil

- 1/4 teaspoon salt

For the Dressing:

- 1 teaspoon lime zest

- 2 tablespoons fresh lime juice

- 1/4 teaspoons salt

- 1/8 teaspoon black pepper

- 1/2 teaspoon dried hot red pepper flakes

- 2 tablespoons olive oil

For the Salad:

- 1/2 pound lump crabmeat

- 1 stalk celery

- 1/2 cup finely diced mango

- 1/4 cup thinly sliced scallions

- 2 tablespoons coarsely chopped fresh cilantro leaves

Instructions

1. Preheat the oven to 375 degrees F. Spray 2 mini-muffin tins with cooking spray.

2. Brush the wonton wrappers with oil, and place each wrapper into a section of a mini-muffin tin.

3. Gently press each wrapper into the tin and arrange so that it forms a cup shape. The wrapper will overlap itself and stick up out of the cup.

4. Sprinkle with salt and bake for 8 to 10 minutes, until browned and crisp.

5. Remove from the tin and allow wrappers to cool.

6. Meanwhile whisk together the zest, lime juice, salt, pepper, and pepper flakes.

7. Add the oil and whisk until well combined.

8. In a medium bowl, toss together the crabmeat, celery, mango, scallions and cilantro.

9. Add dressing and toss to combine. Fill each cup with the crab salad and serve.

Chicken Cordon Bleu Wonton Cupcakes

Chicken Cordon Bleu may make you think of a generic banquet hall buffet, but give this a try and you'll have a change of heart. One thing that Chicken Cordon Blue has gotten right is the combination of smooth cheese and delicious ham

paired with lean, healthy chicken.

Ingredients

- 12 oz (2 ½ cups) cooked diced or shredded

  chicken breast

- 3 oz thinly sliced deli ham, chopped

- 8 wedges of The Laughing Cow Light Swiss

  Cheese Wedges, chopped

- 1 teaspoon mustard

- 24 wonton wrappers

- 6 slices 2% Swiss Cheese, each cut into 4

  equal pieces

- 0.75 oz seasoned croutons, crushed

Instructions

1. Pre-heat the oven to 375. Lightly mist 12 cups in a standard muffin/cupcake tin with cooking spray and set aside.

2. In a microwave-safe mixing bowl, combine the chicken, ham, chopped cheese wedges and mustard and stir together.

3. Place the bowl in the microwave and heat on high for 1 ½ minutes until contents are warm.

4. Use a spoon to mix contents and smush the cheese wedges until they've coated the meat.

5. Push a wonton wrapper into the bottom of each of the sprayed cups in the muffin tin.

6. Using about half of the chicken mixture, spoon evenly into the wonton wrappers.

7. Place one of the 2% Swiss pieces on top of each cup.

8. Press another wonton wrapper on top and repeat the layering steps with the remaining chicken mixture and 2% Swiss cheese.

9. Bake for 10 minutes and remove from the oven.

10. Sprinkle crushed croutons evenly on top of each cup and return the pan to the oven for another 8-10 minutes until the wontons are golden brown and the contents are heated through.

Crunchy Taco Cups

Mexican foods are normally packed with cheese, cream and unnecessary fats. These traditionally calorie dense choices lead to blissful overeating. If you make these taco cups you'll get the best of both worlds: delicious, south-of-the-border taste without the guilt that normally follows.

Ingredients

- 1 lb lean ground beef, browned and drained
- 1 envelope (3 tablespoons) taco seasoning
- 1 (10-oz) can Ro-Tel Diced Tomatoes and Green Chiles

- 1½ cups sharp cheddar cheese, shredded (or Mexican blend)

- 24 wonton wrappers

Instructions

1. Preheat oven to 375 degrees F. Generously coat a standard size muffin tin with nonstick cooking spray.

2. Combine cooked beef, taco seasoning, and tomatoes in a bowl and stir to combine.

3. Line each cup of the prepared muffin tin with a wonton wrapper.

4. Add 1.5 tablespoons taco mixture. Top with 1 tablespoon of cheese.

5. Press down and add another layer of wonton wrapper, taco mixture, and a final layer of cheese.

6. Bake at 375 for 11-13 minutes until cups are heated through and edges are golden.

Skinny Meatloaf Muffins with BBQ Sauce

This one is just in time for summer! No need to kick the bbq for good when options like these delicious muffins are in the cards. Using lean turkey or ground beef makes it a no-brainer for the health-conscious and the foodie alike.

Ingredients

- 1 package (~1.25 pounds) 99% fat-free ground turkey breast
- ½ cup bread crumbs
- 1 cup onions, finely diced
- 1 egg
- 2 tablespoons Worcestershire sauce
- ½ cup barbecue
- ¼ teaspoon salt
- Fresh ground pepper, to taste

Instructions

1. Preheat oven to 350 degrees. Coat a regular (12-cup) muffin pan with cooking spray. Set aside.

2. **To make bread crumbs:** Toast 1 slice whole wheat or multigrain bread. Place in a blender and pulse until made into crumbs.

3. In a large bowl, add ground turkey, bread crumbs, onions, egg, Worcestershire sauce, ½ cup barbecue sauce, salt and pepper.

4. Using your hands or a large spoon, thoroughly mix together until well blended.

5. Add meatloaf mixture to the 9 muffin cups, flattening out the tops.

6. Top each meatloaf muffin with ¾ tablespoon barbecue sauce and spread evenly over top.

7. Bake for 40 minutes. Run a knife around each muffin to loosen it from pan.

8. Remove to a serving plate.

Chicken Broccoli Alfredo Wonton Cupcakes

When you want a healthy meal it normally won't include creamy Alfredo at any capacity. Luckily you're reading this recipe and will love how it can fit easily into your bariatric diet whether you are maintaining your current weight or are still on your journey to your goal weight.

Ingredients

- 1 ½ teaspoons olive oil
- 1 cup broccoli florets, chopped small
- 2 cups cooked shredded or diced chicken breast
- 1 cup light Alfredo sauce
- ½ teaspoon Italian seasoning
- 1/8 teaspoon black pepper
- 24 wonton wrappers
- 1 ½ cup shredded 2% Mozzarella cheese

- 1 tablespoon grated Parmesan cheese

Instructions

1. Pre-heat the oven to 375. Lightly mist 12 cups in a standard muffin/cupcake tin with cooking spray and set aside.

2. Pour the oil into a skillet and bring over medium heat.

3. Add the broccoli and cook for 5 minutes or until broccoli is tender, stirring occasionally.

4. Transfer the broccoli to a mixing bowl and combine with the chicken, alfredo sauce, Italian seasoning and pepper. Stir until well combined.

5. Push a wonton wrapper into the bottom of each of the sprayed cups in the muffin tin.

6. Using about half of the chicken mixture, spoon evenly into the wonton wrappers.

7. Sprinkle about half the Mozzarella cheese evenly over the top of each cup.

8. Press another wonton wrapper on top and repeat the layering steps with the remaining chicken mixture and Mozzarella cheese.

9. When complete, sprinkle ¼ teaspoon of Parmesan cheese over the top of each wonton cup.

10. Bake for 18-20 minutes until golden brown.

Meatloaf Muffin with Mashed Potato Frosting

While this one is a different play on the cup-cake you must give it a chance. If you like the staple of meatloaf and mashed potatoes you'll love every perfect bite of this healthy pairing.

Ingredients

For the Meatloaf Cupcakes:

- 1.3 lb 93% lean ground turkey

- 1 cup grated zucchini, all moisture squeezed dry with paper towel

- 2 tbsp onion, minced

- 1/2 cup seasoned breadcrumbs

- 1/4 cup ketchup

- 1 egg

- 1 tsp kosher salt

For the Skinny Mashed Potato Frosting:

- 1 lb (about 2 medium) Yukon gold potatoes, peeled and cubed

- 2 large garlic cloves, peeled and halved

- 2 tbsp fat free sour cream

- 2 tbsp fat free chicken broth

- 1 tbsp skim milk

- 1/2 tbsp light butter

- kosher salt to taste

- dash of fresh ground pepper

- 2 tbsp fresh thyme

Instructions

1. Put the potatoes and garlic in a large pot with salt and enough water to cover; bring to a boil.

2. Cover and reduce heat; simmer for 20 minutes or until potatoes are tender.

3. Drain and return potatoes and garlic to pan. Add sour cream and remaining ingredients.

4. Using a masher or blender, mash until smooth.

5. Season with salt and pepper to taste.

6. Meanwhile, preheat the oven to 350°.

7. Line a muffin tin with foil liners.

8. In a large bowl, mix the turkey, zucchini, onion, breadcrumbs, ketchup, egg, and salt.

9. Place meatloaf mixture into muffin tins, filling them to the top, making sure they are flat at the top.

10. Bake uncovered for 18-20 minutes or until cooked through.

11. Remove from tins and place onto a baking dish.

12. Pipe the frosting onto the meatloaf cupcakes and serve.

Sesame Chicken Wonton Cups

Chicken doesn't have to be boring and bland. Don't forget the sesame seeds and the cilantro to really make this one stands out.

Ingredients

- 8 ounces boneless, skinless chicken breast
- cooking spray
- 24 wonton wrappers, about 6 oz.
- 2 tablespoons tahini
- 2 tablespoons soy sauce or tamari sauce
- 2 tablespoons maple syrup
- 2 tablespoons mayonnaise
- ½ cup thinly sliced snow peas

- ½ cup shredded carrot

- ½ cup thinly sliced scallions

- 2 tablespoons chopped basil and/or cilantro

- black sesame seeds for garnish, optional

Instructions

1. Place chicken breast in a medium skillet and cover with cold tap water.

2. Place over high heat and bring to a simmer.

3. Reduce heat to maintain a gentle simmer and cook until the chicken is no longer pink in the center and cooked through, 8 to 12 minutes, depending on thickness of the meat.

4. Remove the chicken and let cool. Cut chicken into small cubes.

5. Meanwhile, Preheat oven to 350°F. Coat two 12-cup mini-muffin tins with cooking spray.

6. Cut corners off wonton wrappers to make an octagonal shape.

7. Gently press wrapper down into each cup. Lightly spritz wrappers with cooking spray.

8. Transfer the pans to the oven and bake until the wrappers are starting to turn golden brown and are crispy and bubbling, 10 to 14 minutes. Let cool completely.

9. Whisk tahini, soy or tamari, maple syrup and mayonnaise in a medium bowl until smooth.

10. Stir in the chicken and refrigerate until cold, 40 minutes to 1 hour.

11. Stir snow peas, carrots, scallions and herbs into chicken mixture.

12. Divide chicken salad among wonton cups, about 2 scant tablespoons each.

13. Garnish with sesame seeds, if using.

14. Serve immediately.

Chicken, Bacon and Ranch Wonton Cupcakes

This recipe brings all of your favorite flavors together in a tight, organized package. Light ranch seasoning, bacon and lean chicken breast make this an unbeatable option for healthy eating.

Ingredients

- 1 lb uncooked boneless, skinless chicken breasts
- 1 tablespoon ranch seasoning
- 2 teaspoons canola oil
- 5 slices center cut bacon, cooked crisp and chopped

- ¾ cup yogurt-based ranch dressing (such as Bolthouse Farms)

- 24 wonton wrappers

- 4 oz 2% shredded sharp cheddar

Instructions

1. Preheat the oven to 375. Lightly mist 12 cups in a standard muffin/cupcake tin with cooking spray and set aside.

2. Place the uncooked chicken strips into a Ziploc bag and sprinkle with the ranch seasoning.

3. Seal the bag and shake/massage until the chicken is coated with the seasoning.

4. Bring the canola oil over medium heat in a medium-sized skillet.

5. When the oil is hot, add the chicken pieces and stir them around to coat with oil.

6. Arrange them into a single layer and cook for 5-7 minutes, flipping occasionally, until the chicken strips are cooked through.

7. Remove the chicken to a cutting board and chop into small pieces.

8. Place the chopped chicken into a mixing bowl and stir in the chopped bacon and ranch dressing until well combined.

9. Push a wonton wrapper into the bottom of each of the sprayed cups in the muffin tin.

10. Using about half of the chicken mixture, spoon evenly into the wonton wrappers.

11. Sprinkle about half of the shredded cheddar evenly over the top of each cup.

12. Press another wonton wrapper on top and repeat the layering steps with the remaining chicken mixture and shredded cheddar.

13. Bake for 18-20 minutes until the wontons are golden brown and the contents are heated through.

14. Remove the muffin tin from the oven and allow to cool for 2-3 minutes before removing from the tin

Black Bean and Corn Salad

Simple Black Bean and Corn Salad is a fresh, colorful mix of black beans, corn, bell pepper, avocado and onion, in a light, tangy dressing that is healthy, delicious and easy to make.

Ingredients

- 1 cup corn, whole kernel
- 2 cans (16-ounces each) black beans, rinsed and drained
- ¼ cup parsley, chopped fresh
- 2 tablespoon red onion, minced
- ¼ cup balsamic vinegar
- 2 tablespoon olive oil

- 1 teaspoon lemon juice

- 1 teaspoon garlic, minced

- 1 teaspoon honey or brown sugar

- Dash salt

- ¼ teaspoon ground black pepper

Instructions

1. Mix fresh corn, black beans, red onion and fresh parsley together in a large mixing bowl.

2. Whisk together balsamic vinegar, olive oil, lemon juice, garlic, honey, salt and pepper.

3. Pour over black beans and corn mixture.

4. Let the salad marinade for 30 minutes before serving.

Yogurt Breakfast Popsicles

These easy yogurt popsicles are packed with fresh berries and granola, making them a tasty frozen breakfast to enjoy on-the-go on busy mornings.

Ingredients

- 1 cup Greek yogurt, plain, non-fat

- ½ cup milk 1% or skim

- ½ cup regular or instant oats

- 1 cup mixed berries or chopped fruits

Instructions

1. Mix together the milk and yogurt.

2. Divide the mixture between your popsicle molds.

3. Place a few berries into each mold.

4. Divide the ½ cup oatmeal among each mold.

5. Place a wooden ice cream stick into each mold and place the popsicles into the freezer for at least 4 hours before eating.

6. To remove the popsicles, run the mound under a little hot water until they come loose.

Spicy Peanut Vegetarian Chili

Have you ever thought beans and peanut butter could not go together in harmony? Well, they do, in this satisfying vegetarian chili.

Ingredients

- 1 tablespoon peanut oil (or canola oil)

- 1 cup chopped onion

- 2 cloves garlic, minced

- 2 tablespoons chili powder

- 1 teaspoon chipotle chili pepper (optional)

- ¼ teaspoon dried oregano

- 1 can (16 ounce) black beans, drained and rinsed

- 1 can (16 ounce) white beans, drained and rinsed

- ⅔ cup powdered peanuts

- 1 can (28 ounce) diced tomato

- 1 can (15 ounce) tomato sauce

- 2 cups vegetable broth

Instructions

1. In a large Dutch oven, heat oil over medium high heat.

2. Add onion and garlic, sautéing 3 – 4 minutes or until tender.

3. Stir in chili powder, pepper, oregano and salt.

4. Sauté 2 minutes or until fragrant.

5. Add beans, corn, powdered peanuts, tomatoes, tomato sauce and broth.

6. Bring to a boil.

7. Reduce heat and simmer for about 30 minutes.

Good Morning Casserole

This easy good morning casserole is simple to make, and always a crowd-pleaser!

Ingredients

- 4 slices of bread, crust trimmed
- 1½ cups of egg substitute
- 1½ cups skim milk
- 4 slices cooked turkey bacon, crumbled
- ¼ cup (1 ounce) shredded reduced-fat cheddar cheese
- ¼ cup (1 ounce) shredded reduced-fat Swiss cheese
- ½ cup sliced mushrooms

- ¼ teaspoon seasoned salt

- ½ cup frozen hash brown potatoes, thawed

Instructions

1. Across bottom of lightly greased 9x9 inch baking dish, arrange bread slices, slightly overlapping. Set aside.

2. In large bowl, beat together egg substitute, milk, turkey bacon, 2 Tablespoons each of cheddar and Swiss cheeses, mushrooms, and salt.

3. Pour mixture over bread slices

4. Sprinkle potatoes and remaining cheese over egg mixture.

5. Cover and refrigerate overnight.

6. Bake, uncovered, in pre-heated 350 degree F oven until lightly browned and knife inserted near center comes out clean (about 40-45 minutes).

Stuffed Zucchini Boat

Stuffed Zucchini Boats are the perfect way to enjoy your fresh summer zucchini! Tender zucchini filled with a silky meat sauce, topped with cheese and baked until tender.

Ingredients

- 4 medium zucchini
- 1 pound ground turkey breast
- ½ cup chopped onion
- 1 egg, beaten
- ½ lbs sliced mushrooms
- 1 large tomato diced
- ¾ cup spaghetti sauce
- ¼ cup seasoned whole wheat bread crumbs
- ¼ teaspoon salt
- ¼ teaspoon pepper
- 1 cup (4 ounces) shredded low fat mozzarella cheese

Instructions

1. Cut zucchini in half lengthwise; cut a thin slice from the bottom of each with a sharp knife to allow zucchini to sit flat.

2. Scoop out pulp, leaving ¼-in. shells. Set pulp aside.

3. Place shells in an ungreased 3-qt. microwave-safe dish. Cover and microwave on high for 3 minutes or until crisp-tender; drain and set aside.

4. In a large skillet, cook ground turkey and onion over medium heat until meat is no longer pink; drain. Remove from the heat.

5. In a large bowl mix together zucchini pulp, beaten egg, spaghetti sauce, bread crumbs,

mushrooms, tomato, salt, pepper, ½ cup cheese and cooked ground turkey.

6. Spoon about ¼ cup mixture into each shell.

7. Sprinkle with remaining cheese.

8. Bake uncovered for 20 minutes at 350º F or until brown.

Creamy Cauliflower Puree

This clean and simple cauliflower purée is made by simmering and then puréeing cauliflower and aromatics in a liquid, like cream or chicken stock.

It delivers a pure cauliflower flavor with a satiny texture.

Ingredients

- 1 large (6 to 7 inches in diameter) head of cauliflower
- 3 cloves of garlic (cooked/steamed with cauliflower)
- 1/3 cup low-fat buttermilk
- 4 teaspoons extra-virgin olive oil
- 1 teaspoon butter, salted
- ½ teaspoon of garlic salt
- ½ teaspoon of black pepper

Instructions

1. Break cauliflower into 2" x 2" pieces (or smaller) and put in large microwave safe bowl with ¼ cup water and 3 whole garlic cloves and cover.

2. Microwave for 5 minutes or until cauliflower is very tender.

3. Use garlic press to crush 3 garlic cloves and add them to food processor.

4. Add cooked cauliflower to the food processor.

5. Add buttermilk, 2 teaspoons olive oil, butter, garlic salt, and pepper.

6. Process ingredients until smooth and creamy.

7. Drizzle the remaining 2 teaspoons of olive oil

    on top and serve.

Spinach Frittata

This flexible vegetarian spinach frittata recipe

makes an easy dinner or crowd-pleasing brunch!

You can add your favorite spices or cheese to

customize it.

Ingredients

- 2 teaspoons vegetable oil

- 1 medium onion, chopped (if tolerated)

- 1 package (10 oz) frozen chopped spinach, thawed and drained

- 1½ cups shredded reduced-fat cheddar cheese

- 4 egg whites

- 2 whole eggs

- ⅓ cup reduced-fat cottage cheese

- ¼ teaspoon cayenne pepper

- ⅛ teaspoon salt

- ⅛ teaspoon nutmeg

Instructions

- Heat oven to 375 degrees. Coat a 9-inch pie pan with vegetable oil spray.

- In a medium skillet, heat oil on medium high. Add onion and cook 5 minutes or until softened.

- Add spinach and cook 3 more minutes, set aside.

- Sprinkle cheese in pie pan. Top with spinach/onion mixture.

- In a medium bowl, whisk egg whites and whole eggs, cottage cheese, cayenne pepper, salt and nutmeg.

- Pour mixture into pie pan over spinach and cheese.

- Bake 30 to 35 minutes or until just set. Let stand 5 minutes.

- Cut into wedges and serve.

Stuffed Cabbage Rolls

This stuffed cabbage rolls recipe is a comfort food classic that is hearty, delicious and simple to make.

Ingredients

- 1 head of cabbage, individual leaves removed

- ⅓ cup brown Minute Rice, or other whole grain of choice

- 1 teaspoon olive oil

- ½ medium onion, diced (if tolerated)

- 2 medium carrots, diced

- 1 pound 93% lean ground turkey

- 2 teaspoons garlic powder

- 2 teaspoons Oregano or Italian seasoning

- 2 cups tomato sauce

Instructions

1. Preheat oven to 350°.

2. Wash and blanch cabbage leaves for 30 seconds to make leaves easier to work with.

3. Prepare rice as directed on package.

4. Meanwhile, in a large skillet, heat olive oil over medium heat.

5. Add the onions and carrots, stirring until slightly soft and caramelized.

6. Add turkey to the vegetables in skillet and cook until browned.

7. Add the powders and seasonings.

8. Combine rice and meat.

9. Place ½ cup of mixture into center of 1 cabbage leaf. Roll up, sealing both ends as you roll.

10. Place cabbage rolls in baking dish seam side down, side by side to prevent them from unrolling.

11. Top the cabbage rolls off with the tomato sauce, letting it spill over to the bottom of the dish.

12. Bake for 35-45 minutes. Let stand for 5-10 minutes before serving.

Spicy Avocado Spread

Mashed avocados meet jalapeno peppers and cilantro in this spicy sandwich spread. Try it on a BBQ Chicken Sandwich.

Ingredients

- 1 ripe, medium-sized avocado

- 2/3 cup white or cannellini beans, rinsed and drained

- 2 generous sprigs of cilantro

- 1 ½ Tablespoons fresh lime juice (1-2 limes)

- ½ green jalapeño, seeds removed and chopped

- ½ teaspoon green Tabasco sauce

- ¼ teaspoon salt

Instructions

1. In a blender or food processor blend all ingredients until smooth and creamy

2. Dip vegetables into spread or use as a topping on chicken

Squash Apple Bake

This is a recipe that combines all the best flavors of fall. Great for a Thanksgiving dinner instead of candied yams.

Ingredients

- 1 medium butternut squash, peeled and cut into ¾ inch cubes

- 2 medium apples, peeled, cored, and cut into thin wedges

- 1 Tbsp Splenda

- 1 Tbsp all-purpose flour

- ¼ cup melted butter

- ½ tsp salt

- 2 tsp ground cinnamon

Instructions

1. Mix squash and apples together in a casserole dish.

2. Combine other ingredients and spoon over squash and apples and mix together.

3. Bake, covered, at 350 degrees F for 50 – 60 minutes, or until tender.

4. If you like a crispier topping, take lid off casserole dish for last 10 minutes of cooking

Cool Ranch Veggie Pizza

This appetizer is a cool pizza made with refrigerated crescent roll dough and topped with finely chopped vegetables. Zucchini, mushrooms, green peppers, green onions and tomatoes all work well as toppings.

Ingredients

- 2 LaTortilla Factory (or other similar) low-carb wraps (large)

- ½ cup reduced fat chive and onion cream cheese

- ½ cup light sour cream

- 1 package Hidden Valley Ranch Dressing (use dry mix)

- ⅛ cup shredded carrots

- ¾ cup raw broccoli

- ¾ cup diced tomatoes

- ⅛ cup diced green pepper

- ⅛ cup diced cucumbers

- ¾ cup Kraft Light shredded Colby & Monterey Jack cheese

- ½ cup sliced black olives

Instructions

1. Mix cream cheese, sour cream, and ranch dressing packet together.

2. Spread evenly on tortillas.

3. Top with veggies and olives and sprinkle with cheese.

4. Cut each tortilla into four pieces and serve.

Spicy Deviled Eggs

Grab a dozen eggs, and get boiling, because these Spicy Sriracha Deviled Eggs are just what your holiday celebration needs! I mean it.

Ingredients

- 6 hard-boiled eggs (You will not use three of the yolks in this recipe)
- 2 Tablespoons of creamy horseradish sauce or Greek yogurt
- ½ teaspoon dill
- ¼ teaspoon spicy mustard (Use Dijon for mild deviled eggs.)
- ⅛ teaspoon salt

- Dash of black pepper and paprika

Instructions

1. Peel the eggs and cut in half lengthwise.

2. Place 3 yolks into a mixing bowl, and set the whites aside. (Save the other three yolks for another use.)

3. Mash the yolks with creamy horseradish sauce or Greek yogurt, dill, mustard and salt.

4. Spoon or pipe filling into egg white halves.

5. Sprinkle with pepper and paprika.

www.ingramcontent.com/pod-product-compliance
Lightning Source LLC
Chambersburg PA
CBHW051344150726
48000CB00003B/1046